TIGER WOODS

TIGER WOODS

A PICTORIAL BIOGRAPHY

by Hank Gola

COURAGE
BOOKS

AN IMPRINT OF RUNNING PRESS
PHILADELPHIA • LONDON

10 9 8 7 6 5 4 3 2 1

Digit on the right indicates the number of this printing.

Library of Congress Cataloging-in-Publication Number 97-68285

ISBN 0-7624-0272-5

Tiger Woods
A Pictorial Biography
was prepared and produced by
Michael Friedman Publishing Group, Inc.
15 West 26th Street
New York, New York 10010

Front and back jacket photographs: ©J.D. Cuban/Allsport
Jacket Design: Kevin Ullrich

Editors: Francine Hornberger and Stephen Slaybaugh
Art Director: Kevin Ullrich
Designer: Charles Donahue
Photography Editor: Wendy Missan
Production Manager: Camille Lee

Color separations by HK Scanner Arts Int'l Ltd.
Printed in China by Leefung-Asco Printers Ltd.

Published by Courage Books, an imprint of
Running Press Book Publishers
125 South Twenty-second Street
Philadelphia, Pennsylvania 19103-4399

For Uncle Ed. Thanks for putting that sawed-off five-iron in my hands so many golf seasons ago.

For Mom. Just thanks.

Contents

Introduction

When Kultida Woods took her young son on a visit to her native Thailand, Buddhist monks put their hands on the youngster and told her that he was special, a gift from the angels. He did not demonstrate his golf swing for them. If he had, they would have had no idea what he was trying to do. Somehow, they knew just the same.

Tiger's father, Earl, once predicted that his son would "change the course of humanity." If he does, it is because of the stark contrast he forms against most every other golf champion. He is the child prodigy who lived up to the promise. He is a role model raised on strict moral values by his parents. He has as much talent as a golfer as anyone who has ever played any sport. With the blood of many races—African, Caucasian, Asian, and Native American—flowing through his veins, he is a new breed of golfer who has brought a previously untapped sector of the American population to the whitest corner of the sports world.

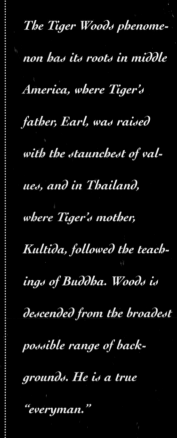

The Tiger Woods phenomenon has its roots in middle America, where Tiger's father, Earl, was raised with the staunchest of values, and in Thailand, where Tiger's mother, Kultida, followed the teachings of Buddha. Woods is descended from the broadest possible range of backgrounds. He is a true "everyman."

Woods could be a golfer "who comes around once in a millennium," said Tom Watson. He also happens to be the perfect golfer for the nineties: a multicultural American with a winning smile and a near-perfect swing. Golf purists love him for the way he plays the game. Others admire him for the pride he has brought to Black and Asian communities. Tiger is one-quarter African-American, one-quarter Thai, one-quarter Chinese, one-eighth American Indian, and one-eighth Caucasian.

As for his ability, a study by Titleist, his ball and clubmaker, found that he "comes closer to achieving optimum launch conditions—a combination of swing speed and angle of impact" — than any of the three hundred touring pros the company has tested over the last twenty years.

Coach Butch Harmon, who worked with Greg Norman for five years, says he "has never seen anything" like Tiger's raw talent. He adds, "Jack Nicklaus, when he came along, was probably the closest to what Tiger is now."

Most refreshingly, he is not perfect. He slams the occasional club into the ground after an errant shot and, every now and then, he'll even rankle a U.S. President. As his caddie, Mike "Fluffy" Cowan, attests, "I have seen him make the same mistakes any twenty-one-year-old kid might make. But I'm not going to tell you about them." It's true that so much has never been expected of an athlete this young, not even Michael Jordan. But few athletes have accomplished as much so soon.

When Woods won the 1997 Masters by a record 12 strokes, he captivated the nation.

Tiger Woods isn't just a young phenom. He has become an absolute phenomenon in himself.

Woods may be better known to the masses for his massive length off the tee but through endless practice, he developed a creative short game that can stack up against any in the world.

The expressive eyes. The expensive swoosh. The expansive smile. If there ever was a golfer made for 1990s television, it's Tiger Woods.

Chapter One

Tiger Cub

iger Woods often says that so many things have been written about his childhood, he can't tell what is true and what isn't.

No wonder. With its coincidences, twists of fate, and miracle moments, Tiger's tale sounds more fantastic than real. But such is the case with genius. As Woods' first golf coach, Rudy Duran, has said, young Tiger is the twentieth-century equivalent of Mozart.

It starts with Earl Woods—"Pop" to Tiger—the man who shaped the legend. Growing up in the heartland of America with a baseball fanatic as a father, Earl was a good enough catcher to have impressed Roy Campanella and to have been offered a contract by the fabled Kansas City Monarchs of the old Negro Leagues. Turning down the dream in favor of his mother's preference for an education, Earl entered Kansas State University, where

Opposite: Just starting out, Tiger Woods was destined for greatness even at the tender age of thirteen. Left: Tiger shows off his trophy won in the USGA Junior Open in 1990.

he broke the color barrier in Big Eight Conference baseball, enduring all the racial hardships of the time.

Earl joined the Army and saw two tours of duty in Vietnam as a Green Beret, earning a Vietnamese Silver Star for a mission conducted through a Vietcong-occupied village. There, his life was saved twice in the same day by a South Vietnamese officer, Lieutenant Colonel Nguyen T. Phong, whom Earl called "Tiger" because he fought like one.

After he left Vietnam and Saigon fell, Woods never heard from Phong again. He feared the worst, knowing Phong's staunch anti-Communist beliefs. But he vowed to honor his friend by naming his next-born son "Tiger."

Not that the odds were great on that happening. Woods, nearing forty, already had two sons and a daughter when the strain of separation and time caused his first marriage to end in divorce. A short

At age fourteen, Tiger was already accustomed to moments like these, when he could contemplate another almost-certain victory. At eight, he won the Optimist International World Junior championship.

From the moment he crawled out of his high chair and took a swipe with his father's 5-iron, Tiger has had the makings of a legendary golf swing. The young face and flashy wardrobe have matured. The follow-through and the concentration have endured.

time later, he was transferred to Bangkok.

An attractive Thai woman named Kultida, "Tida" to her friends, was employed as a secretary in the U.S. Army office in Bangkok. Earl asked her out and admired her spunk. They were married in Brooklyn in 1969. Earl was still stationed in the ancestral home of the Dodgers (and Jackie Robinson) when, about five years later, he had his first introduction to golf.

A fellow officer, knowing Woods' athletic background, kept pestering Earl to join him on the golf course. When Earl eventually agreed, he hacked his way to a 92, accompanied by the cackles of his persistent playing partner. As competitive as he was, Woods promised himself that he would win a return match before his nemesis left the Army—a grand total of six weeks to bring his game up from nowhere.

Believe it or not, three weeks later, Earl shot 81 and won the grudge match at Fort Dix, New Jersey, by 4 strokes. He was also hooked for good on the game that allowed him such sweet revenge. Just as he had vowed to name any future son "Tiger," he promised to introduce golf early on to any child with whom he and Tida might be blessed.

A year later, Earl was a civilian, close to a scratch player, and living with his new wife in an all-white neighborhood in Cypress, California. The welcome wagon didn't exactly race to the Woods' front door. Instead, limes from nearby trees—and BBs—kept passing through their front window.

In his teens, Tiger would rather practice golf than do anything else. If he wasn't on the putting green, working on his stroke, he was in his mother's living room, chipping over and around furniture.

And, oh yes, Earl and Kultida were expecting that child. On December 30, 1975, Eldrick "Tiger" Woods was born.

The name Eldrick was Kultida's creation, a combination of letters from both parents' first names. Earl compromised on that point but added the Tiger part in honor of his never-to-be-forgotten friend. As for Earl's other promise—to introduce golf to his son—that took place in the garage where he built himself an indoor driving range and worked on getting his handicap down to a three.

When Tiger was six months old, Earl would sit him in a high chair in the garage while Earl beat balls into a net. Maybe it took the place of a mobile placed above his crib, but whatever the case, little Tiger was transfixed by his father's swing. You could say he learned by osmosis because a few months months later, Tiger wriggled out of his high chair, grabbed the sawed-down putter that he had been dragging around the house in his walker, and set up a golf ball. With a miniature version of his dad's swing, Tiger's first golf shot was dead solid perfect into the net.

Earl nearly fell over at the sight; he soon realized that he had something special on his hands.

Tiger was his and Tida's to nurture and Earl did not take that responsibility lightly. He didn't want to mess up what he believed to be a gift from God. Using his background as a teacher as well as the common sense his father had used with him, Earl not only began to guide Tiger through the delicate process of becoming the world's best golfer but started to shape his son into a person who would contribute to society as well.

Earl likes to say today that Tiger is a better person than he is a golfer, and he objects to being called an obtrusive stage parent. He once suggested to Tiger that he play Little League baseball. Tiger said it would take time away from his golf. The same applied to girls. Tida, meanwhile, made sure that school came first; homework was completed before Tiger took to the tees to work on his game.

Tiger's first golf hole was played at eighteen months on a 410-yard par-four at the Navy Courses in Los Alamitos, California, where Earl had been taking him to hit balls. He reached the green in 8 and got down in 3. A short time later, when Tiger was two, Tida spread the word of Tiger's ability to Jim Hill, a former NFL player who was working as a sports anchor in Los Angeles. After taping Tiger play a hole at the Navy Courses, Hill predicted that Tiger would be to golf what Chris Evert and Jimmy Connors were at that time to tennis.

That tape led Tiger to an appearance with avid golfer Bob Hope on *The Mike Douglas Show*, where Tiger complained about the unfair break in the makeshift green as both adults howled. Later that year, Tiger won his first tournament—against boys ten and under. A year later, he broke 50 on nine holes for

Tiger took his first golf swing at ten months. By age fourteen, he had the swing of a true champion.

the first time, shooting a 48 from the red tees. Soon, he was hustling quarters on the putting green until Earl made him stop.

Rudy Duran, Tiger's first coach, came into the picture when Tida happened upon Heartwell Golf Park, a par-three course which she figured would be a good place for a four-year-old to play. Duran was the resident pro and asked to see Tiger hit a few balls. He was blown away by Tiger's natural ability as well as his skill level.

"The first time I saw Tiger hit a golf ball, I saw a kid who'd popped out of the womb as a Magic Johnson or a Wolfgang Amadeus Mozart," Duran recalls. "He had talent oozing out of his fingertips, and you just couldn't wait until he grew up to see how good he could be."

From then on, the feats became more and more incredible. At age six, Tiger already had a pair of holes-in-one. He wowed clinics by hitting all varieties of shots: cuts, knockdowns, you name it. At seven, he

almost beat a club pro and showed up Sam Snead in a two-hole exhibition conducted on the seventeenth and eighteenth holes at Soboba Springs Country Club.

Snead had offered Tiger a mulligan when the boy hit his first shot to the edge of a pond. But Tiger always played and counted every shot. He knocked it out of a soggy lie, took a bogey on the hole, and lost to the Slammer by a stroke.

By now, the mental side of Tiger's game was also taking form. His father had introduced him to sublimi-

nal tapes. Messages of strength and discipline could be picked up below the music of flutes and the sound of babbling brooks and ocean sprays. The kid loved them so much that he listened to them constantly and tacked messages onto his bulletin board such as: "I focus and give it my all" and "I smile at my obstacles."

Earl would also use his special-forces training as inspiration to strengthen Tiger's mental toughness. When he played a round with his son, he would move or jingle coins on Tiger's back swing, rip open the

Velcro on his glove while Tiger putted, purposely improve his own lies in the rough, shave strokes— anything to unnerve him. But Tiger was as unflappable back then as he was at the Masters.

"[Earl] knew all about those psychological debriefings...because he is an ex–Green Beret and he had to go through all of that," Tiger explained. "He would bring me to the edge and then back off. After about six months, he would try to do it and I would just laugh at him because it didn't work anymore."

By the time Tiger was eight years old, he was already being conditioned to winning. He captured the first of five Optimist International Junior World golf championships and started to think of far-off horizons. His idol was Greg Norman, who had established himself as the world's best golfer by winning the 1986 British Open. Tiger also cut out a chart of Jack Nicklaus' accomplishments that had appeared in

Tiger poses with his proud father, Earl, after winning his first USGA Junior Open title at age sixteen.

Jack Nicklaus, a former child prodigy as well as one of Tiger's idols, respects and admires Tiger's talent.

Golf Digest. It was a timeline barometer of greatness and the blueprint for Tiger's early career. Not only had Woods decided to meet Nicklaus' records to gauge his own success — he decided to break them. And break them, he did.

Nicklaus was nine years old when he first broke 50 for nine holes. Woods had done it at the age of three. Nicklaus first broke 80 on eighteen holes at twelve, Woods at eight. Nicklaus won his first U.S. Amateur Championship at nineteen, and his first Grand Slam event at twenty-two. Woods was well on his way.

Woods takes a swing dur-
ing the USGA Open tour-
nament that would present
him with his first big victo-
ry in his amateur career.

Tiger Woods ● *29*

Chapter Two

2

Amateur Career

Sixteen-year-old Tiger Woods played in his first PGA Tour event, the Nissan Los Angeles Open, in February 1992, at the plush Riviera Country Club. Three days later, he toted his own bag at a scruffy public track in La Mirada, shooting 37 over nine holes in the rain to help Western High School beat Gahr High School. Curious reporters, accustomed to roomy press tents, followed him in a pickup truck.

For the rest of his amateur career, Woods would be pulled between these divergent poles. As his game progressed, it was certain that he was headed for professional golf, but the nurturing of Tiger as both a player and person had to come first.

One year, for instance, Woods passed up a chance to defend his state high school championship to play in sectional qualifying for the U.S. Open. The following year, he

Opposite: Tiger competes for the 1996 Amateur Champion title in Cornelius, Oregon, in August 1996. Left: The Eisenhower Amateur World Team Championship, Paris, France, 1994.

Woods contemplates his next move during the Honda Classic.

passed up the U.S. Open sectional qualifying to attend his high school graduation.

Before his sophomore year at Stanford University ended, Woods had won three straight USGA Junior Amateur Championships, followed by three consecutive U.S. Amateur titles. He had played in the 1995 and 1996 Masters, the 1995 and 1996 U.S. Opens, and the 1995 and 1996 British Opens, and had joined Phil Mickelson and his benchmark, Jack Nicklaus, as the only three players ever to win the NCAA championship and the U.S. Amateur in the same year.

Since 1993, Woods' swing was being polished by Butch Harmon, who originally put Woods on a three-year plan. Woods had a good idea that "Tigermania" was only going to grow. The only question in his mind was how soon would he outgrow amateur golf.

Whether winning another tournament, working in the classroom at Stanford, or posing at Versailles during a break from the Eisenhower Amateur World Team Championship, near Paris, Tiger can always feel as though he's on top of the world.

Woods lines up a shot at the U.S. Amateur Championship in Newport, Rhode Island, 1995.

As it turned out, Woods' prelude to the PGA Tour was a short bridge that he crossed with expected ease. Only the legendary Bobby Jones, who never turned pro, had a more sparkling amateur career, simply because he never renounced his amateur status.

Tiger took the American Junior Golf Association circuit by storm. By the time he was fourteen years old and a high school freshman, he had already shot par fours with his driver. In one AJGA event, the Big I in Houston, he was paired with the long-hitting but still obscure John Daly, who was one of the twenty pros brought in to compete with the juniors on the final day of the event. Early in the day, Daly was heard saying, "I can't let this thirteen-year-old beat me." If Daly hadn't birdied three of the last four holes, it would have happened.

Tiger swings during the 1992 LA Open. Although he did not play his best game in this event, he would not let himself give up on golf.

The 1992 LA Open.

In 1991, Tiger's career hit fast forward. The highlight was his first USGA championship in the Junior Amateur, where he defeated Brad Zwetschke, 1 up. He was fifteen years old, the youngest victor in the forty-four-year history of the event, and it earned him an exemption into that summer's U.S. Amateur, where he failed to advance into match play. Still, the young man was being noticed, by both the professional tour and agents representing professional golfers.

Earlier in 1991, Woods barely missed qualifying for the LA Open, the tournament he had watched closely his entire life. Two spots were open for 132 players, and Tiger, who had holed out for eagle at the seventh hole, was still in contention when he got to eighteen, needing to eagle the par five. His tee shot, however, came to rest on a bare spot of a downslope. He went for the green anyway, but, with the impossible lie, he plunked the ball into the pond in front of the green. Tiger finished with a 69. The two spots went to Mac O'Grady and John Burckle, who each shot 66.

Ron Hinds, who played Woods that day, told reporters that he was actually rooting for Woods to make it.

"You try to avoid envy in golf but that kid humbled all of us. I was hoping he'd get into the tournament so that I could watch this awesome kid play against Kite and Crenshaw and those guys. After seeing Tiger play, you can't help but wonder what might have been," he said.

In April of 1991, Tiger met Jack Nicklaus for the first time. Jack was giving a clinic in Southern California, and Woods was there to show off his swing. After taking his first look at the fluid fifteen-year-old, Nicklaus told him, "Tiger, when I grow up, I want to have a swing as pretty as yours."

In December, the International Management Group, which had hired Earl Woods to scout junior golfers, invited Tiger to Isleworth in Orlando, Florida, to spend some time playing with a few of their clients. There, young Tiger impressed the likes of Mark O'Meara, as well as his own idol, Greg Norman, who was amazed that "the young whippersnapper" was outdriving him. About the same time, Tiger received an invitation from Nissan to play in the 1992 LA Open without having to qualify. There, followed by the largest galleries of the first two days, he disappointed himself by shooting 72–75 and failing to make the cut.

"Give me time to grow and I'll be back," he declared.

Of course, if Woods couldn't yet measure up to PGA Tour standards, he could still demoralize his peers. When Tiger had what he called his "A-game" going, he was unbeatable. Take for instance the highly regarded Pacific Northwest Amateur in 1994, where he played 26 holes in 13-under to close out his opponent, 11 and 10. But perhaps more impressive were the times when Woods staged a series of remarkable comebacks to win. He confounded his opponents by wearing them down, physically and mentally, proving that he could grind when necessary, a trait he'd need on the PGA Tour.

In his first Junior Amateur final, he was down three holes after six, and when he won an unprecedented second straight Junior Amateur in 1992, he was two down with six left against Mark Wilson. Although he was medalist by 4 shots and blew away his first four opponents, Wilson proved a tough foe. All even at the eighteenth hole, Woods won with a bogey to Wilson's double. The match was so draining that he broke into tears.

For his third Junior Amateur, Tiger had to survive a dormie situation in the final: he was down two holes with two to play against sixteen-year-old Ryan Armour. Not at his physical peak due to a bout with mononucleosis, Woods birdied the seventeenth and eighteenth holes to pull even and won the match with par on the first extra hole.

"It was the most amazing comeback of my career," he said at the time. "I had to play the best two holes of my life under the toughest circumstances and I did it."

Armour had rolled in a forty-foot putt to go 1 up on fifteen, and when Woods lipped out a four-footer on sixteen, the deficit was 2. Armour figured that two pars would win him the title, but Woods hit a 9-iron within eight feet on seventeen, then told his caddie and sports psychologist Jay Brunza, "Got to

be like Nicklaus, got to will this in the hole." He topped that with a ten-foot birdie putt on eighteen, and Armour, stunned that two pars weren't good enough to finish off Tiger, three-putted the first extra hole from sixty feet.

A pattern was established. In the 1994 U.S. Amateur at TPC Sawgrass, Woods was 6 down after thirteen holes of his thirty-six-hole final match with Trip Kuehne, an Oklahoma State junior and a good friend. Tiger admitted, "He put a number on me," after Kuehne's morning round of 66. After all, no one had ever come back from six holes to win a U.S. Amateur, but Woods was sure that enough holes remained for him to make up the gap.

Still 5 down with twelve holes left, the deficit was reduced to 3 when they made the turn. At the sixteenth, Woods' birdie evened the match for the first time in thirty-three holes. They would go to seventeen, one of the most famous par-threes in the world with its island green. Woods had only one thought—go for the pin, even though it was dangerously to the green's far right side.

With steel nerve, Woods pulled out a wedge and hit a soft fade into a right-to-left wind, to the right of the flag, a shot so risky that few pros would attempt it, especially under these circumstances. The ball hit four paces from the edge of the water in the fringe and spun back, three feet from the water, fourteen feet

(continued on page 44)

The first of his three straight U.S. Amateur championships was won in 1994 at TPC Sawgrass, where Tiger came from six holes down to beat his good friend Trip Kuehne. With the pressure on, Woods won the match by hitting an incredible wedge shot into the island green of the seventeenth hole.

Previous pages: Tiger takes a time-out to rethink his game during the 1995 Amateur Championship. Right: Woods and a caddie line up a putt on the seventeenth green.

from the cup. He'd have to make the putt, but the match was over. "I was in a zone," he explained later.

"It's an amazing feeling to come from that many down to beat a great player," Woods exclaimed. "It's indescribable."

Woods' second Amateur title felt even better because his game had become more complete. At his first Masters, earlier that year, Woods had struggled with the distance control of his irons. Augusta National, a second-shot golf course, made him work

on that facet of his game, and his appearances at the Scottish and British Opens that summer gave him a chance to test his shot making. The U.S. Amateur at Newport Country Club is where it all came together.

Tiger's opponent in the final was George "Buddy" Marucci, a forty-three-year-old investment consultant and owner of a luxury car dealership. It was this type of cunning, career-amateur opponent who had always given Woods the most trouble in match play, because they used their experience to save par from impossible places and were never fazed by the mystique that he had already created.

Marucci had Woods down by 3 after twelve holes and 2 after nineteen. When they reached the thirty-sixth hole, Woods had built a one-hole lead but Marucci was on the green with a twenty-foot birdie putt that could have tied the match. Woods was back on the eighteenth fairway, where he decided to punch an 8-iron, a shot he had practiced over and over since Augusta.

He calculated 140 yards of flight. He was off by 18 inches, the ball spinning back toward the pin. When Marucci missed his putt, he conceded Tiger the match.

A jubilant Earl, drinking champagne that his son was still not legally old enough to sip, made a proclamation outside the old clubhouse after the event: "Before he's through, my son will win fourteen major championships."

Woods hopes for victory after making a shot during the 1995 U.S. Amateur Championship.

Even for Tiger Woods, golf can sometimes be a lonely game. Here, at the back edge of a huge bunker, Woods is lost in concentration, in a "zone" that only the best players visit.

A traditional hug from "Pop" after Tiger won his second straight U.S. Amateur, at Newport Country Club in 1995. Woods rallied to beat forty-three-year-old car dealer Buddy Marucci in the final.

3
Chapter Three

Pro Beginnings

The decision to leave the safe haven of Stanford University to venture into the madness that awaited him in the world of professional golf was more thought-consuming for Tiger than the decision to attend Stanford in the first place. Stanford is no powerhouse in NCAA golf, but coach Wally Goodwin took an early interest in Tiger. He never put on a dog and pony show to lure him there, however. In fact, when Woods made a recruiting visit to Stanford, he slept on a dorm floor.

Most significantly, Stanford was unique in the educational opportunities it offered for Tiger and the fact that no matter how extraordinary Tiger Woods was as a golfer, his fellow students were just as extraordinary in their chosen fields. Woods didn't stick out at Stanford. He fit in.

Opposite: Woods competes in the Greater Milwaukee Open, Glendale, Wisconsin, August 31, 1996. Left: The PGA Tour Championship, Tulsa, Oklahoma, October 25, 1996. Tiger didn't know exactly what was in store for him his first months on the PGA Tour — his only goal was to earn his playing privileges for next year. He was sure, however, that he had outgrown the amateur phase of his career.

Swing coach Butch Harmon makes a point to his prize pupil. As he made his decision to join the PGA Tour, Woods respected Harmon's opinion above all others. Harmon assured him that not only would he compete, he would win.

Woods could treasure the time spent on the driving range with his Stanford teammates, inventing and executing shots, and he could play without needing uniformed security officers to keep galleries moving and at bay.

Still, the fact remained: Woods had outgrown college and amateur golf. He was bored. Two events in July demonstrated that. First, he was eliminated in the first round of the Western Amateur by nineteen-year-old Terry Noe, the 1994 Junior champ. "I was just flat, and that told me something," Woods explained. But when he competed against the best players in the

world at the British Open, he shot a second-round 66. He needed more of a challenge.

"Something really clicked that day, like I had found a whole new style of playing," he said. "I finally understood the meaning of playing within myself. Ever since, the game has seemed a lot easier."

Woods sought out the opinions of several touring pros, including Fred Couples, Ernie Els, Curtis Strange, and Greg Norman, who told him he was ready, physically and mentally. Butch Harmon, whose opinion on golf Tiger respected most, assured him that he could not only compete but win. Tiger also knew

Earl Woods sits behind his son as Tiger officially announces his professional debut at the Greater Milwaukee Open. Seen as overbearing by some but not by the only person who counts, Earl guided his son into and through his amateur golf career with a firm but loving hand.

Under the media spotlight since his appearance on The Mike Douglas Show at age three, even Tiger had to be surprised by the unparalleled attention he received as a professional. But on the course, executing a shot, Tiger was still in his own world.

that to develop fully, he had to work on his game full time. At Stanford, there were exams and papers, often just before and after tournaments.

Woods would be no average rookie on tour. He didn't have to play to make a living; he could play to win golf tournaments. His winnings would almost be incidental, compared with the endorsement contracts he signed with Nike for apparel and Titleist for equipment. Nike head Phil Knight likened Tiger's marketability to that of Michael Jordan, his most famous

Woods reads a difficult green at the 1996 U.S. Open at Oakland Hills, outside Detroit. The narrow fairways and thick, rough and slick greens of Open venues still remain unsolved for the young pro. Although Grand Slam talk began immediately after the rousing Masters victory, Tiger didn't come close to challenging in the last three '97 majors.

client and one of Tiger's idols. Tiger would fly in chartered jets and take up residence at Isleworth in Orlando to avoid California State income taxes. But Harmon knew that his prodigy would face a different kind of pressure.

"All the amateur titles Tiger has won won't mean anything, and he'll have to prove himself in a hard environment where there is no mercy," he said. "He's got the intelligence and the tools to succeed very quickly. My only worry is that he's losing two of the best years of his life to do something that is very

demanding for a young person. Considering everything, he's making the right decision, but he's going to have to grow up faster than I'd like him to."

Woods reached his final decision just before the U.S. Amateur after careful consultation with the people closest to him. In doing so, he altered his original plan.

"I had intended to stay in school, play four years at Stanford and get my degree, but things change," Woods told *Sports Illustrated* about his decision to leave school. "I didn't know my game was going to progress to this point. It got harder to get motivated for college

matches, and since I accomplished my goal of winning the NCAA, it was going to get harder still. Finally, winning the third Amateur in a row is a great way to go out. I always said I would know when it was time, and now is the time."

Woods was also going in at full tilt. When he first started leaning toward becoming a professional, he had intended to enter two tournaments as an amateur and, if he won either, he would use the two-year exemption to turn pro. If he didn't, he would return to Stanford for his junior year. Now, he would use sponsors' exemptions to play in seven tournaments over the final two months of the Tour season. If he got himself into the top 125 on the 1996 money list, he'd have an exemption the following year. If he won any of those, the exemption would be for two years. If neither occurred, he would have to qualify for the 1997 Tour by earning one of the forty or so spots available at the dread PGA Tour Qualifying Tournament—"Q-School" for short—which he said he didn't "want to fool with."

The Greater Milwaukee Open, a few days after his emotionally draining conquest of Steve Scott, provided the coming-out party. The news leaked early so that Woods was forced to issue a brief statement confirming his decision a day before the scheduled press conference. Someone counted nine Nike swooshes on his person when he played in the Pro-Am on Wednesday, but it was only part of the makeover. For the first time,

The U.S. Open, Bloomfield Hills, Michigan, June 3, 1996. Galleries aren't always on top of Tiger. Far from the ropes and the front lines of Tigermania, he slides in a putt.

Steve Scott, a major rival of Woods', competes during the 1996 U.S. Amateur Championship.

he was announced as "from Orlando, Florida." Toting his Titleist bag was veteran caddie Fluff Cowan, ostensibly on loan from Peter Jacobsen, who was recuperating from back woes. A few weeks later, Cowan would officially end his eighteen-year relationship with Jacobsen, who took it well.

"Mike has an opportunity to work for probably the greatest thing to happen to golf in the last twenty years," Jacobsen said.

For the record, Woods' first shot as a paid professional soared 336 yards down the right side of the fairway. On six, a par-five, he drove 330 yards and hit a 5-iron 226 yards to within 12 feet of the pin. He sank that for his first eagle as a pro. His first round was a

67, 8 shots out of the lead. He wouldn't win the tournament, but he would make the cut and record his first ace on the PGA Tour—the ninth of his life—with a 6-iron on the 222-yard fourteenth hole on Sunday.

The crowd let out a sustained roar that didn't ebb until Woods finished his walk from the green to the fifteenth tee.

"It was wild," he recounted. "They didn't have to do it. It was a good shot that happened to turn out perfect."

Tiger's final round of 68 tied him for sixteenth and earned him his first paycheck—$2,544.

Over the next several weeks, Woods' journey into professionalism had its peaks and valleys. He finished

Tiger takes a divot out of the fairway on a three-quarter shot into the green. Woods climbed up the leader board with each of his first professional events. He barely lost the Quad Cities Classic to the stocky, short-hitting Ed Fiori.

Right and opposite: Woods at The Greater Milwaukee Open, August 1996.

eleventh at the Bell Canadian Open, which was short-ened to fifty-four holes by rain, and he missed a chance to win his first tournament at the Quad Cities Classic, played at the PGA Tour outpost of Coal Valley, Illinois. The field there was minus most of the Tour's best players, who were competing in the President's Cup in Manassas, Virginia. That week, and when Tiger took a one-shot lead into the final round, much of the media scurried to the airport.

They would be disappointed.

On the fourth hole of the final round, Woods was attempting to fade his drive back to the fairway. Aiming left, he actually hooked the shot into a pond.

After a penalty stroke, Tiger's recovery shot hit a tree and caromed back into the same water. He would take 8 on the hole, losing a 3-shot lead, and although he was still tied for the lead on seven, a 4-putt fin-ished him off.

The tournament went to Ed Fiori, a stocky, short-hitting, forty-three-year-old tour veteran.

"It was kind of like the rat snake getting the cobra," Fiori quipped.

Tiger tied for fifth for $42,150.

"I'm pretty pissed off," he said in the press tent. "But I will tell you one thing. The way I look at it is I broke in at Milwaukee and did okay. I did better in Canada. Today, I not only broke the top ten barrier, but the top five, too. That's progress."

At the B.C. Open in Endicott, New York, Woods improved to a tie for third in another rain-shortened tournament. But he also irked the winner, Fred Funk, by stating that he still gave himself a good chance to win even though he was 6 strokes off Funk's pace going into Sunday.

At the Las Vegas Invitational two weeks later, Funk blasted the brash newcomer.

"Everything has been Tiger, Tiger. They kind of forget about everyone else out here," said Funk, who cited Tiger's comments as inspiration for shooting a first-round 63.

Funk went on to say he "took offense" at Tiger's remarks at the B.C. Open.

Woods competes in the Mercedes Championship at LaCosta Resort in Carlsbad, California, in January of 1997.

Woods flashes a grin in the press tent after winning his first PGA Event, the Las Vegas Invitational, where at twenty years, ten months, and seven days old, he became one of the youngest Tour winners ever. By breaking through, Tiger assured himself of a Tour exemption in 1997.

"He [Tiger] failed to mention he was six shots back on the last day. No one was going to catch me that day, not even Tiger Woods."

Funk's attitude was more representative of the type of PGA Tour pro who had gradually earned his way up the ladder. Athough the resentment from career grinders was to be expected, the more accomplished players on tour seemed less offended by the attention and endorsement money Tiger was receiving.

Between Endicott and Las Vegas, Woods was committed to play the Buick Challenge in Pine Mountain, Georgia. While he was there, Tiger was supposed to receive the Fred Haskins Award, college golf's equivalent of the Heisman Trophy. On Wednesday, he played a nine-hole practice round with Jacobsen, Davis Love III, and Jeff Sluman and decided that he was too "mentally exhausted" to play the tournament. In just four tournaments, Woods' $140,194 in earnings had vaulted him into 128th place on the money list, three spots away from where he needed to be to automatically earn his PGA Tour card for the 1997 season. The Buick Challenge was unnecessary, and he decided to withdraw from the event and skip the dinner. Tournament sponsors, who had laid

Tiger's great length is a product of shoulder and hip speed. Shown here during his first professional victory at the Las Vegas Invitational, the power is about to be uncoiled near the top of his backswing. Note how the left shoulder is tucked perfectly under the chin.

Woods takes a satisfying
swing at the Mercedes
Championship on
January 11, 1997.

out $30,000 for the dinner, had to cancel the affair, inconveniencing many who had traveled hundreds of miles to attend.

Prominent tour pros were now outspoken in their criticism of Tiger, including Fred Couples, Davis Love, Curtis Strange, Tom Kite, Larry Mize, and Peter Jacobsen.

"Everybody has been telling him how great he is. I guess he's starting to believe it," Love remarked.

"This tournament was one of seven to help him out at the beginning when he needed help to get his card," Strange said. "How quickly he forgot that."

"I don't ever remember being tired when I was twenty," said Kite.

Tiger tried to repair the damage he had caused. He sent letters of apology to each person who had planned to attend the dinner and further apologized in *Golf World* magazine.

"I am human. I do make mistakes," he pleaded.

He realized that he should have attended the dinner and left afterward. As it turned out, the decision to miss the tournament was best for his golf game.

The Las Vegas Invitational is a five-round event played on different courses each day, none of them particularly difficult. Woods opened with a 70, but with four more rounds to play, he had more than enough golf left to make up the deficit. He shot a masterful 63, followed by a 68 and a 67. He capped that off with a 64 on Sunday. Although Davis Love caught

him from behind on the eighty-eighth hole, he was unable to birdie either of the last two holes, and the two were set for a playoff.

For Woods, it was a familiar match play situation. He had won eighteen consecutive matches in collecting his three Amateurs, and he used his match play experience on the first sudden-death hole.

Love hit first with a drive and split the fairway. Woods could have driven past him but chose a 3-wood instead and finished a few yards behind. Hitting first from the fairway, Tiger put the pressure on Love with a good approach shot, which landed 18 feet from the pin. Love accelerated a bit too much with his 7-iron and his shot came over the top, flirted with the water, and found the back bunker. He blasted out 8 feet past the pin while Tiger lagged to within 2 feet. Love missed. Tiger rolled in the winner.

"We were all trying to prolong the inevitable," said a gracious Love. "We knew he was going to win. I just didn't want it to be today."

Tiger Woods became one of the youngest winners ever, at twenty years, ten months, and seven days. (Ray Floyd won the St. Petersburg Open when he was twenty years, six months, and thirteen days old in 1963. Phil Mickelson won the 1991 Northern Telecom Open while still an amateur, at twenty years, six months, and twenty-eight days old.)

And it took only two months for Woods to win again. He finished third at the La Cantera, Texas

Open before beating Payne Stewart by two shots to win the Walt Disney World Oldsmobile Classic.

Woods' first seven tournaments now stood as the greatest stretch of golf in fourteen PGA Tour seasons. He was the first player with five straight top five finishes since Strange in 1982, and of his last twenty-one rounds, he had broken 70 in eighteen of them, including eleven of the last twelve. He finished the year twenty-third on the money list with $734,790.

As for his ongoing pursuit of Nicklaus, Woods was again ahead of the Bear. Nicklaus had no victories and just one top ten finish in his first seven tournaments as a pro. Tiger had two wins and three other top tens.

"I haven't really played my best golf yet," he said as he headed for the Tour Championship, which took the top thirty money winners.

Perhaps his A-game would have surfaced there, if not for an unexpected setback. Earl, who had kept up a cigarette habit and poor diet despite quadruple-bypass surgery ten years earlier, suffered a mild heart attack after the first round of the tournament. A worried Tiger shot himself out of contention with a 78 the following day.

Earl would eventually require further open-heart surgery in 1997, the year Tiger added to his victory list the Mercedes Championship, where he became the youngest player ever to surpass $1 million in career earnings.

The Mercedes brings together the champions of every PGA Tour event from the previous year, and fittingly, it came down to a playoff between Woods, the runaway 1996 Rookie of the Year, and Tom Lehman, the 1996 Player of the Year and British Open champion. Woods birdied the last four holes Saturday to shoot 65, making up four shots on Lehman and tying him for the lead at 14-under. When rains hit LaCosta on Sunday, Woods and Lehman were two of six golfers unable to begin their final rounds. Play was suspended and tournament officials waited two hours before canceling the round. So the two men, arguably the two best players on the PGA Tour, headed out to battle in a sudden-death playoff, starting at the par-three seventh.

Anticipating eighteen holes with Tiger after the third round, Lehman had been eager to match his game against the rookie's.

"I don't know how good Tiger Woods is.... Tom Lehman is Player of the Year, but Tiger is probably the player of the next two decades," Lehman remarked. "Hopefully, I can play my very best. If I do and lose, I'll know there's a new kid in town."

Unfortunately, the playoff proved anticlimactic. Lehman misjudged the wind and his tee shot landed in the water to the left of the green. Woods could play safe to the middle of the green now. He hit a 6-iron to the right of the hole, and it spun back to within a foot of the cup.

Kultida "Tida" Woods embraces her son after his victory at the Mercedes Championship.

Right and Opposite: Woods competes in the AT&T Pebble Beach National Pro-Am tournament, February 2, 1997.

"I was lucky I drew number two," he said. "If it's a clear, sunny day, it's an advantage to hit first. But under the conditions today, I had the advantage. I didn't know what the wind was doing. I watched his ball ride the wind."

That didn't mean that Woods considered himself an underdog. "In my own mind, I'm always the favorite," he said. "This is what I set out to do. It's not surprising if you win when you have your mind set from the start of the week that you're going to win."

Woods tied for eighteenth place at the Phoenix Open, where Tigermania was in full force. When he aced the sixteenth hole at the Tournament Players Championship (TPC) at Scottsdale, the huge gallery erupted as if it was at a basketball game, littering the place with cups and wrappers. A week later, Woods finished in a tie for second as Mark O'Meara won his fifth AT&T title at Pebble Beach.

From there, Tiger headed for Asia and Australia. In Thailand, where most people don't know a golf ball from a grapefruit, Tiger was treated as a national treasure. And when Kultida said she hoped her son would marry a Thai woman, it made national headlines.

Woods dominated the field at the Asian Honda Open, winning by 10 strokes, despite being so sick from food poisoning during the Pro-Am that he had to walk off the course in the middle of his round.

Along with all this, Tiger's thoughts were divided between golf and his father, who was scheduled to undergo open-heart surgery within the next month.

By April, Earl was well enough to attend tournaments again.

Chapter Four

The Masters

T he origins of golf are ancient enough to be attributed to Roman soldiers. Trace the written history of the game, and you will inevitably arrive at Old Tom Morris, patron saint of the Royal and Ancient Golf Club of St. Andrews.

In 1862, at Prestwick Golf Club on Scotland's rugged west coast, Old Tom sealed away the second of his four victories in what would one day be called the British Open. His crude clubs included a cleek and a long nose. The ball he played was made of gutta-percha. He wore a woolen coat and a thick black beard as shields from the harsh elements. In three rounds over the twelve-hole Prestwick course, he whipped the field by 13 shots.

Opposite and left: Tiger's runaway victory at the 1997 Masters came on just his third trip to Augusta. Symbolically, however, it was much longer in coming. Lee Elder, the first black player to be allowed into the Masters, would call the Sunday of Woods' victory at Augusta, "a glorious day."

Not many competitors thought that Tiger Woods could master the subtleties of Augusta National in just his third Masters appearance. But as he played his first practice round, shown here, on Tuesday, he could still feel the momentum of the 58 he had shot at his home course the previous week. "I'm tournament tough," he boasted.

Augusta National, with its sweeping fairways and lack of rough, was made for Tiger Woods. He likened it to "a driving range, bombs away." Rather than stepping back to a safer 3-wood or 1-iron, Woods could take the driver and hit it for all it was worth, turning par-fives into par-fours.

Old Tom, as one might expect of a patriarch, was also among the foremost architects, greenkeepers, club makers, and teachers of his day. His brightest pupil was his own son, Young Tom, a prodigy who hit the ball longer and played more boldly than anyone who had come before him, including his father. Beginning at age seventeen, Young Tom won four consecutive Open championships with scores that were miraculous for the time. In the 1870 championship, just eight years after his father's victory at Prestwick. Young Tom's thirty-six-hole total of 149 (13 better than his father's last winning score) translated into a stroke average not to be equaled until the invention of the rubber-cored ball. His margin of victory was 12 shots.

Another view of the jubilant Woods on the eighteenth green Sunday. The final hole was more of a tester than it should have been. A photographer clicked his camera as Woods was striking his tee shot, causing him to pull the ball far left, to the members' driving range. It was but a slight detour to the green.

Sadly, Young Tom died of a burst blood vessel in his lung on Christmas Day of 1875. He was only twenty-four years old. Because his death came so shortly after he had lost both his wife and baby during childbirth, the romantic notion is that Tom perished from a broken heart. His grave marker at St. Andrews, to which even rival Englishmen contributed, has always been a monument to unfulfilled promise. Before his death, Young Tom had played golf on a level his contemporaries had not thought possible.

While the Old and Young Toms were busy golfing, America was busy with something else. The Civil War raged, and in some places blood was spilled on future fairways. In Augusta, Georgia, the heart of the Confederacy, a sprawling indigo plantation was converted into a nursery called The Fruitlands.

Things are said to change slowly around Augusta. In this case, it took some 130 years, until Eldrick Tiger Woods brought symmetry to an unsolved, ancient equation.

The Fruitlands plantation is now the sacred ground of the Augusta National Golf Club, where a young phenom, groomed by his father, and born one hundred years and five days after Young Tom Morris died, played golf on a level his contemporaries had not thought possible. He assaulted and surpassed the tournament record shared by Jack Nicklaus and Raymond Floyd with a seventy-two-hole total of 270, 18 strokes under par. His 12-shot victory margin was the largest

in a major championship since Young Tom's 127-year-old triumph, second only to Old Tom's 1862 record. On top of all this, Tiger became the first minority golfer to win a major at a golf club that had not admitted a minority to its membership until 1990. The club's founder, an iron-handed bureaucrat named Clifford Roberts, had proclaimed, "As long as I'm alive, golfers will be white, and caddies will be black."

Another ironic piece of history, the year 1997 was the twentieth anniversary of Roberts' suicide on the Augusta grounds. Woods was not yet two years old when Roberts, suffering from terminal cancer, ended his own life with a bullet to the head. But Tiger was on his way toward his destiny. If he was born to win any golf tournament, it was this one.

When he arrived at the storied setting for his third Masters and his first major as a professional, the anticipation was intense—and mixed. Ladbrokes of London had him as one of the betting favorites at 10-1 odds but there was also some skepticism over his chances. For all of Woods' length, Augusta National was always considered a second-shot golf course. Of all the Masters champions, only Nicklaus, a six-time winner, had ever overpowered the layout. The others won by guile, nerve, and steady hands on the diabolically fast greens.

In his two previous Masters, Woods had not done a good job of thinking his way around the golf course, where each shot must be set up like billiards. It came as no surprise. Nick Faldo said it took him "half a

Woods with another short iron in his hands. All week long, Tiger never hit anything longer than a 7-iron into any green. Jack Nicklaus, who once overpowered golf courses in the same manner, enthused that Tiger was "making this golf course melt away."

dozen" Masters before he "got the gist" of Augusta. The field respected Woods' extraordinary talent but expected the course to have the final say again, at least this year.

Woods' game was not at its best, either. His irons had not been sharp leading up to the Masters, including his most recent tournament two weeks earlier, the Tournament Players Championship at Sawgrass. In finishing 17 strokes behind the winner, Steve Elkington, Woods was forced to scramble for pars.

Although he amazed the swollen galleries with his creativity around the greens, birdies aren't made by getting up and down on par-fours. Yet, as he spoke to

reporters after his final round, Woods was confident that he could work out the flaws in a week of intense practice with Butch Harmon. Writers scribbled down the quotes, hardly paying attention.

"I'm tournament tough this time," Woods told them. "Coming to the Masters will be a lot different this time. I'll be ready to play. I won't have to pull all-nighters getting ready for finals while everyone else practices. I was at a disadvantage then. Now the tables are turned."

A few days later, that golf game came together in a sudden burst. He and Mark O'Meara were sharing a practice round at Isleworth, their home course in

Tiger enjoys a lighter moment with his caddie, Mike "Fluff" Cowan, his protector and chief counsel on tour life. Without Cowan's intimate knowledge of the golf course, Woods would have been ill-prepared to pull off his record victory.

Orlando. Playing from the tips, Woods shot a round of 59 that left him ecstatic over his game but disappointed in his score. Woods was 10-under-par through ten holes, but he failed to birdie two par-fives on the front nine that could have made his round even lower.

"He should have shot 57," said an awestruck O'Meara. "It was a pretty easy 59. I know it sounds crazy. It wasn't like he was out there bombing them in and chipping in from everywhere. I think his longest putt was 16 feet."

LEADERS
HOLE 1 2 3 4 5 6 7 8 9 10 11 12 13 14 15 16 17 18
PAR 4 5 4 3 4 3 4 5 4 4 4 3 5 4 5 3 4 4
WOODS
ROCCA
STANKOWSKI
KITE T.
WATSON T.
SLUMAN
LOVE
LANGER
COUPLES
TOLLES
17
18
4

As impressive as the round was—only two players have ever broken 60 in competition—it was still unofficial. And Isleworth isn't Augusta. Few thought it an omen. The rule of thumb still made experience a large factor. At his first press conference of the week, Tiger tried to convince the golfing press that he was ready to win now.

"Is it realistic?" Woods said, repeating a reporter's question. "I think so. I don't know if anyone else does. If things go my way, I might have a chance to win this tournament.

"You've got to be at a level where you feel confident in your abilities, physically and much more importantly, mentally," he added. "This golf course is going to test every facet of your game."

Also confident was Nick Faldo, the three-time Masters winner. Tradition pairs the defending Masters champion with the defending U.S. Amateur champion for the first round of play, and this promised to be as close to a match play situation as Thursday can get.

Playing with Faldo can be nerve-wracking, as Greg Norman experienced in his final-round collapse in 1996. The Englishman is meticulous, nearly robotic. When he's on, he is so steady, so consistent, that he can pressure an opponent's every shot. Totally into his own game, he scarcely says a word to his playing partner. He was also perfectly capable of playing head games, and though Woods dismissed this kind of tension, he still played nervously.

Faldo had honors off the tee, splitting the fairway. Woods paused to recognize the ovation, then yanked his drive into the evergreens that line the left side of the hole. As he walked toward his lie, he had a perfect view of Faldo's straight back and his caddie, Fanny Sunesson. One shot into the tournament and he was already walking in Faldo's wake.

It is said that you can't win a golf tournament on the first day, but you can lose it. For the first nine holes, Woods was on his way to shooting himself out of contention. So for that matter, was Faldo, who was not putting the pressure on anybody but himself this day. In fact, Faldo was showing signs of succumbing to the distractions of Tiger's gallery. They tended to shuffle after Woods hit, leaving Faldo to constantly ask for quiet. Three-putting three greens, he made the turn in 41. Woods, who kept missing fairways, was only one better. Even a portion of their gallery deserted them to look for better golf.

Standing in the gallery, Tiger's swing doctor, Butch Harmon, remarked that the kid was suffering through a case of the jitters. Take the eighth hole, for instance. Woods' drive dove deep into the left woods, leaving him 20 yards from the fairway, the ball resting on pine needles. He had to escape from a predicament that placed a brigade of trees between him and safety. Tiger put his left foot on a 6-inch curb and his right on the cart path. His opening was a small, square window through the trees. The shot never even ticked a leaf.

Woods watches his final putt drop on the eighteenth hole Sunday. Woods' score of 270 was a Masters record, and his winning margin was the largest ever in a 72-hole Major.

"When I looked at it initially, I thought I could go through the trees on the left-hand side," Woods said. "Then I saw a little gap when I looked a little more right. I took the chance and tried to go through this gap, hit the shot, and it went right through."

The crowd, hungry for heroism, roared. But Woods missed the green and settled for bogey on a hole that could have been a round-killer.

As Woods approached the tenth tee, his tournament was in the balance. At that point, he had never played a Masters round under par and he was 4-over for his first nine holes of 1997. He needed to learn from the front side quickly. When he reached into his bag for a 2-iron to hit off the tee, the student was about to become the teacher.

"On the tenth tee box," he would say later, "I finally decided to play some golf."

A sweet swing produced a shot down the middle of the fairway. A 9-iron left him 15 feet away —his first birdie. On twelve, he chipped in for a birdie on the par three—two straight.

"It was a little 9-iron bump-and-run shot that rolled right in," Woods later admitted. "That really got me going."

Another birdie followed on the par-five thirteen, then a 10-foot save at fourteen.

By the fifteenth hole, Tiger was Tiger again. It was back to the driver for a 349-yard tee shot and a 151-yard wedge to within 4 feet of the cup. He dropped

Tiger had taken all the suspense out of the golf tournament by Sunday. Still, Earl told him it would be the toughest round of his life from an emotional standpoint. All that was left for Masters patrons to watch was his assault on the tournament records. Here, he tees off on the third hole.

Above and opposite:
The 1997 Masters
tournament tested
Tiger's reserves of
character, imagination,
and skill.

that for an eagle as a train whistle was heard in the background. Someone said it was the sound of a new era in golf. Three holes later, he had a chance to tie the Augusta National back-nine record of 29 set by Mark Calcavecchia in 1992, but just missed his birdie putt on eighteen.

The bigger headlines went to John Huston that day for holing out a 5-iron from off the eighteenth fairway for an eagle that gave him a short-lived first-round lead. But Tiger was only 3 strokes behind.

"I was absolutely horrible out there early on," he said. "I was pretty ticked off after the front nine. I couldn't do anything out there. The fairways are pretty big here, but I sure couldn't hit them. I was all over the place....I knew what I was doing wrong, so it was getting out of that and trusting the motion."

As for Faldo, even a strong back nine of 34 left him with a 75. Afterward, he appeared a beaten man. "He played great," Faldo said through a blank expression. "He got his score back together. Good luck to him."

Opposite and left: Two different follow-throughs in two different rounds at Augusta. Woods talked a lot about playing his "A-game." As the rest of the field would discover, the kid is practically unbeatable when he does.

Woods didn't need luck. On Friday, he followed up his opening-round 70 with the best score of the second round, a 66, launching drives to places no one had ever hit the ball before. He averaged 336.5 yards off the tee, missed only one fairway, and needed only 29 putts.

He played the four par-five holes in 5-under, with the kind of short-iron approach shots most players hit into par four holes. He hit a short iron into the 555-yard second and nearly drove the third green from 360 yards.

As dazzling as that was, Woods put on an even more impressive power display on the back. On thirteen, Woods hit a 3-wood and an 8-iron into the 485-yard hole and made an eagle from 20 feet. He drove 350 yards on number fifteen, hitting a wedge from 150 yards to 8 feet for a two-putt birdie. In between, he birdied number fourteen after hitting a 115-yard sand wedge to 3 feet. Obviously, Thursday's butterflies had scattered.

"I felt very comfortable with my game," Woods said. "I was very relaxed and very patient."

Tiger reminded everyone that, "I came here to win the tournament." People were starting to believe him. The raves came from everywhere.

Nicklaus, who used to intimidate opponents with his length, said that Woods "reduces the golf course to nothing. I mean, that's the thing people used to say about me," Nicklaus went on. "I'm sitting down there

(continued on page 94)

Tiger watches the flight of the ball out of a bunker on the first hole of the final round. Woods admitted to nerves as he started the day. He was able to get this shot close enough to save par.

playing 9-irons and 8-irons and everyone else is back there with 3-irons and 2-irons and I'm sort of laughing, saying, 'Boy, this is a tough course, huh?'

"I'm going to tell you one thing," Nicklaus said. "It's a shame Bob Jones isn't here. He could have saved the words for me in '63 for this young man because he's certainly playing a game we're not familiar with....With his power, he's making this golf course melt away."

The only question was whether Woods could face up to the weekend pressure. Colin Montgomerie, the seasoned European pro sitting 3 strokes back in second place, was hoping to apply it. Paired with Woods for Saturday's round, he issued a polite but unmistakable challenge.

"It all depends on Mr. Woods," Montgomerie stated. "The way he is playing, this course tends to suit him more than anyone else playing right now. If he decides to do what he's doing, well, more credit to him. We'll all shake his hand and say well done. But at the same time, there's more to it than hitting the ball a long way. The pressure is mounting more and more. I have more experience in major golf than he has. Hopefully, I can prove that."

Woods fully expected to feel a little heat on Saturday, which is called "moving day" by the players because it sets up Sunday's stretch run. He also expected to withstand it. The surprise of the third round, however, wasn't that Woods continued along

but that the rest of the field faded away. Clearly, Tiger was demoralizing the golfing world, including Montgomerie.

"I told my pop this morning that somebody was going to make a run, shoot a 66 at worst," said Woods, who set his goal at no bogeys for the round. He didn't want to provide anyone with even a crack of daylight. Then he went out and shot the 65 himself—without making bogey on any hole.

"Everybody was trying to birdie every hole to try to catch up to him," said Davis Love, who started the day 7 strokes back, shot 72, and fell 14 strokes behind. "That's a difficult way to play."

Paul Stankowksi, who shot a fine 69 on Saturday only to lose 4 more strokes, lamented that, "every time I looked up it was like, 'Oh, he made another birdie. Oh, he made another birdie.' Tomorrow, there's no chance unless I shoot 57."

The tournament that people say begins on the back nine Sunday was over after the back nine Saturday. Woods went out in 32, upping his lead on the Scotsman Montgomerie. After five holes, the 3-shot difference was a 7-shot difference. At the par-five second, Woods birdied and Montgomerie bogeyed. At the par-five fifth, Woods dropped a 10-foot birdie putt while Montgomerie failed to get up and down from out of the bunker.

Montgomerie disposed of, Woods later capped his round off by putting enough backspin on a sand

The youngest and first minority winner of the Masters lets his emotions out after ending with a par on the seventy-second hole. Even as Tiger played the final stretch after Amen Corner and neared the inevitable conclusion, he never lost his sharp focus. A young boy reached out to pat him on the shoulder after he hit from outside the ropes on fifteen, but Tiger later said he hadn't noticed him.

Tiger-watching was the only thing to do on Sunday. If you could get close enough or claim one of the natural vistas conceived by Bobby Jones and Alistair McKenzie when they laid out Augusta, you could glimpse Woods' determination as he marched toward the green jacket.

wedge to spin it back out of the short rough around the green to within a foot of the cup for a tap-in birdie. That left Woods at 15-under-par, 201 after fifty-four holes, 9 strokes ahead of Costantino Rocca, 10 better than Stankowski, and 11 in front of venerable pros Tom Kite and Tom Watson.

Montgomerie's 74 pushed him 12 shots back. He was now talking the talk of concession.

"All I have...is one brief comment," Montgomerie humbly announced. "There is no chance humanly possible that Tiger Woods is going to lose this tournament. No way."

Reminded that Norman blew a 6-stroke lead and lost by 5, Montgomerie noted with stinging candor, "This is different, this is very different. Nick Faldo's not lying second for a start and Greg Norman's not Tiger Woods."

After what had happened to Montgomerie, Rocca was not about to suggest the kid might choke.

"I can win maybe if I play [only] nine holes—and under par, too," he said sheepishly.

Asked if Tiger was catchable, Watson simply replied, "No."

He's a boy among men and he's showing the men how to play," Watson observed. "He's got the heart of a lion."

Even Kite, the only player to remotely give himself a chance, admitted, "He's driving us crazy; he's really doing some incredible stuff."

Older, more experienced competitors Colin Montgomerie (left, top) and Constantino Rocca (left, bottom) ultimately proved no match for the twenty-one-year-old phenom, Tiger Woods, in the 1997 Masters Tournament.

Woods, meanwhile, said he was interested only in hanging a green jacket in his closet, not obtaining the records that were within his reach. That night he would sleep soundly, but his father would tell him that Sunday's round would be the toughest he'd ever play in his life. He meant it from an emotional standpoint. Earl also told Tiger it would be the most rewarding.

Earl Woods knew there were twenty-one years invested in those eighteen holes. From his first swing in diapers, young Tiger was raised for that moment, to crash through the barriers of country-club policy, unbreakable records, and classic golf architecture. There would be no duel down at Amen Corner this day, not unless Tiger forsook every fiber of his make-up. No, this would be a grand coronation.

Two days later was the Fiftieth Anniversary of Jackie Robinson's Major League debut, and for these two events, minority fathers and grandfathers put their kids and grandkids in front of the television for a lesson in history and pride. Likewise, Lee Elder, the first black player ever to compete in the Masters in 1975, made his way down from Atlanta to be part of the congregation. "It's a glorious day," Elder said, after visiting with Tiger on the putting green before the round. "I was part of history by being the first black to play here. I had to be part of history by watching Tiger be the first black to win here."

Black workers at Augusta National went about their duties with an extra spring in their step. This golf course had been a place of magic for so many players in the past. It would now turn 130 years of history on its ear.

With his play on Sunday, Tiger would shape that history. If there were nerves, they surfaced early. The great Ben Hogan's record of consecutive holes without a bogey was spared when Woods made his first in thirty-seven holes on number five as he hit his approach into the sand and couldn't save par. He took another bogey at number seven when he hooked his ball into the Georgia pines and could only run his approach into a greenside bunker, where he again failed to get up and down for par.

Rocca had the deficit down to 8 after Woods' first transgression, but that lasted about ten minutes,

whereupon the Italian bogeyed six himself. Rocca wasn't up to heroic challenges this day—he would balloon to a 75. It was Tiger and Augusta, one on one, one last time.

On eight, Woods found his nerve again by working his way out of trouble. After he hooked his approach into the woods, the ball settled on a bed of pine needles with a mound blocking his view of the flagstick. Montgomerie had made bogey from the exact same spot playing with Woods the day before. But Woods played a perfect bump-and-run up the slope and the ball trickled to within 4 feet. The birdie seemed to settle him down.

It wasn't until sixteen that Woods started thinking about the tournament record. His focus had been that sharp all week long. On fifteen, when he had to hit to the green from outside the ropes, he didn't even notice a young boy who rushed up to him to pat him on the shoulder.

"I knew I had to get through Amen Corner with par at worst," he said. "I couldn't afford to let up on my concentration. All you have to do is put a couple of balls in the water and there goes the landslide.

"After I got by the [last] water hole—sixteen—I knew that it was pretty much over because I could bogey in."

Even on eighteen, Woods tried hard not to let the reception disrupt his concentration. A photographer clicked too early, while Woods was in his backswing,

and he hooked his tee shot way left into the members' driving range. Perhaps it was fate because it allowed him to interact with his adoring gallery.

Woods got to the ball first as the marshals parted the crowd, but his caddie, Mike Cowan, was off getting a distance reading. Woods jumped up and down, looking for him over the various heads, when the crowd began to chant as if they were at a basketball game.

"Fluff. Fluff. Fluff."

Calmly, the iron shot found the green. One more par for the tournament record. He stood over his ball and shook his head in disbelief. Two putts later, it was his. He pumped his fist, hugged Fluff and headed off to the back of the green, where his parents were waiting. "We did it," Earl Woods, two months out of heart surgery, told him. "I love you and I'm so proud. Now let it out." So Tiger cried.

"He's been talking about winning the Masters since he was five years old," said Earl. "I told him he

"We did it!" Earl tells his son. "I love you and I'm so proud." Earl had nearly died during the second of two heart operations two months earlier and this victory was an emotional moment for the whole family.

had to grow up first....It's wonderful to see someone achieve his dream."

Faldo draped the green jacket on Wood's shoulders and said, "Phenomenal performance. Welcome to the green jacket."

The rout was over. At twenty-one, Tiger was the youngest Masters champion ever and the youngest to win a major since twenty-year-old Gene Sarazen won both the U.S. Open and PGA Championship in 1922. Woods' score of 270 was a Masters record and his winning margin was the largest ever in a seventy-two-hole major.

He played the four par-five holes in 5-under for the week and never hit anything longer than a 7-iron into a par four green. From the time he arrived at the tenth

The previous year's champion, Nick Faldo, helps Tiger on with his green jacket. Woods had gone head-to-head with the stoic Brit in the first two rounds, but none of Tiger's playing partners — not Faldo, not Montgomerie, not Rocca — could unnerve him that weekend.

A little hardware for his collection. It's a replica of the Augusta National clubhouse, the former mansion of an indigo plantation, where Tiger stayed as an amateur participant his first two Masters tournaments.

tee after a shaky start Thursday, Woods played the final sixty-three holes 22 under par. In the middle thirty-six holes—when he put the tournament away—Woods hit 26 of 28 fairways—93 percent of them. He was not only close to the greens, but in a perfect position to do something with it.

"I've never played an entire tournament with my A-game. This is pretty close—sixty-three holes," Woods said later.

Even more remarkable was the effect Woods had on his playing partners. Faldo, Paul Azinger, Montgomerie, and Rocca averaged 74.25 strokes for the round they played with Woods and were totally dispirited after that. Faldo shot 81, Azinger 77, and Montgomerie 81 on the subsequent days.

Fellow pros were even talking about the need to add trees, rough, length—anything to toughen up the course for Tiger so that he doesn't run away with the Masters each year.

"The rest of us will just be teeing it up for silver medals for the next twenty years," said third-place finisher Tommy Tolles.

Even Tiger couldn't do his performance justice with words. He said he hoped his victory would open doors for minority golfers. He hoped kids would start playing the game because they thought it was "cool."

He paid homage to the black pioneers of the sport, such as Elder, Charlie Sifford, and Ted Rhodes.

"Those are the guys who paved the way. All night I was thinking about them, what they've done for me and the game of golf," he said. "Coming up on eighteen, I said a little prayer of thanks to those guys. Those guys are the ones who did it."

He said he never dreamed he'd win the Masters in this fashion.

By the end of the interview session, reporters were asking him about some serious business, like whether he thinks he will be the greatest golfer the world has ever seen.

"I know my goal is to obviously be the best," he said carefully. "I know that's a pretty lofty goal but I expect nothing but the best for myself. I think as time goes along, hopefully that will happen."

Four days earlier, it would have sounded like cockiness. After Augusta, no one was arguing.

Chapter Five

The Impact, The Future

I t was almost five o'clock Friday at the Players Championship, and Tiger Woods was well on his way to a mediocre seventy-two-hole total of 1-over-par, which would leave him 17 shots behind Steve Elkington's winning score.

Whether Woods was in contention or not did nothing to diminish the size or hysterics of his gallery, which had just marveled at the colossal drive he had just scorched off the sixteenth tee.

Off to the side, almost inconspicuous by comparison, stood Jacksonville Jaguars coach Tom Coughlin. "I had to see him drive," Coughlin confessed.

At the same time, two women, wearing less than standard golfing attire, began shrieking at Woods as if he were John, Paul, George, or Ringo.

Woods hoped that his Masters victory would break barriers and attract a new generation of golfers. "I hope kids will think that golf is cool," he said.

The demeanor that Woods adopts to shield himself from media attention is broken down when he's with his friends or at his Tiger Woods Foundation clinics with kids. "That's where he lets down his guard and has a lot of fun," says his former business manager, friend, and one-time Stanford teammate Jerry Chang.

"Happy hour is kicking in," cracked one of the burly volunteers specially assigned to escort Woods from green to tee.

"You're not kidding," Woods replied.

For Tiger, it was just another day at the office — another six or seven hours of negotiating what has come to be known as Tigermania. PGA officials estimate that the presence of Woods generally doubles the attendance at any tournament, bringing in many first-time fans. A Generation X of sorts, they are younger and more racially diverse than the typical golf watcher, and they flock to their hero like others once did to Arnold Palmer and Jack Nicklaus.

Take Joyce Jones, a retired black woman from New York, a phone-company worker for thirty years, who had just retired to a condo on Amelia Island before the TPC.

"I know it's strange coming from someone who's retired but Tiger's my hero, too. That man inspires me. He gives me vision," she said as she made her way along the fairways.

As a result of Woods' emergence, more and more young people from inner cities are now looking to golf. His clinics, run through the Tiger Woods Foundation, have been filled to capacity. In between

(continued on page 113)

Where Tiger goes, crowds follow. Tiger's youth and diverse ethnic background have attracted new fans to the game of golf. It is to be hoped that talented players of all backgrounds will emerge in the future, inspired by Tiger's achievements.

hitting shots, including a few back over his head, he stresses the importance of education and family.

His friend, Jerry Chang, a Stanford teammate who lives with him and has served as his business manager, says that the real Tiger comes out when he works with kids.

"That's where he really lets down his guard and has a lot of fun," Chang said. "That's where the questions are, 'Do you have a girlfriend?' or 'What do you eat for breakfast?'" Maybe Woods enjoys the clinics most because the kids don't make demands.

Take an incident at the TPC, where he spent a half-hour in the autograph tent but was booed because he didn't satisfy the entire line, which seemed to stretch forever.

Said Cowan, "There were thirty-five to fifty-year-old men knocking kids out of the way so they can get an autograph. I find that quite strange."

And even some who would seem to welcome his arrival on the golf scene are almost bitter about it.

Noting that Jim Thorpe is the only other African American on tour, Bill Spiller, Jr., sees Woods only as a marketing symbol. It was Spiller's father, a great black player, who forced the PGA to revoke its "non-Caucasians clause" in 1961, fourteen years after Jackie Robinson first played for the Dodgers.

Opposite: Tiger answers reporters' questions at a press conference after the Nissan Open in Pacific Palisades, California, February 1997.

Left: Fluff tries to keep things loose for Tiger during a round, like here at the Buick Classic at Westchester Country Club. Tiger is an expressive player and his face usually reflects his feelings about a round.

Woods on the practice range at the PGA Championship at Winged Foot Golf Club in Mamaroneck, New York, joking with his swing coach Butch Harmon.

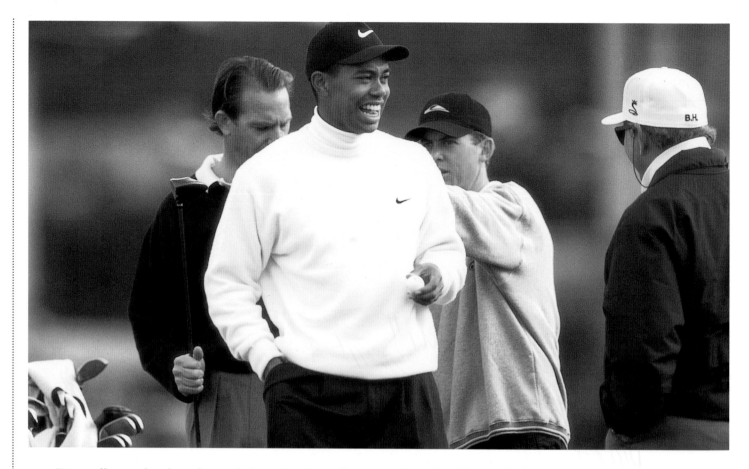

"You tell me what has changed since the days of my father? Nothing," Spiller said in an interview in the *Los Angeles Times*. "Tiger Woods? He has nothing to do with it. He has light-brown skin, no Negroid features, not the sort that white Americans find so offensive. He is not a threat.... He is somebody corporate America can gloat on, feel good about, but it's not real."

Woods doesn't renounce his African-American heritage, but at the same time, he does not want to be depicted as a "black golfer" because he feels it disregards his Asian mother's heritage completely. He is indebted to men like Charlie Sifford and Lee Elder who faced racial bias in no uncertain terms in their day.

Woods' father has always reminded him of that history, and when Tiger played the Masters for the first time, he made a side trip to the Forest Hills Golf Club, a public course, where he met with the forgotten black caddies of Augusta National. Woods staged a clinic for kids at Forest Hills and spent a good deal of time with the men who were pulling hardest for him.

"It's a black thing," Earl Woods told reporters on the scene. "We are acknowledging that we know who came before Tiger and that they suffered humiliation. It's a way of saying thank you and a promise to carry the baton." At that point, Earl upped the stakes.

"We need a Technicolor green jacket, a black in a green jacket," he said. "It is time. The day has come and it's long overdue. I promise you it will happen."

When it did in 1997, it seemed like only the start.

Woods lines up his shot at the AT&T Pebble Beach National Pro-Am competition on January 30, 1997.

A triumphant moment,
Woods scores a hole in one
on sixteen during the 1997
Phoenix Open.

Bibliography

Books

Andrisani, John. *The Tiger Woods Way: Secrets of Tiger Woods' Power Swing Technique.* New York: Crown Publishers, 1997

Eubanks, Steve. *Augusta: Home of the Masters Tournament.* Nashville: Rutledge Hill Press, 1997

Plumridge, Chris. *The Illustrated History of World Golf.* New York: Exeter Books, 1988

Rosaforte, Tim. *Tiger Woods: The Making of a Champion.* New York: St. Martin's Press, 1997

Sifford, Charlie, with James Gullo. *Just Let Me Play.* Albany, New York: Briton American Publishing, 1992

Strege, John. *Tiger.* New York: Broadway Books, 1997

Wartman, William, *John Daly: Wild Thing.* New York: Harper Paperbacks, 1996

Woods, Earl, with Peter McDaniel. *Training a Tiger.* New York: HarperCollins Publishers, 1997

Articles

Casaday, Laurie. "All Want to See Tiger's Stripes," *The Florida Times-Union*, March 30, 1997

Crothers, Tim. "Tiger Woods: Golf Cub," *Sports Illustrated*, March 25, 1991

_____. "No Holding This Tiger," *Sports Illustrated*, August 9, 1993

Diaz, Jaime. "Encore! Encore!" *Sports Illustrated*, September 4, 1995

_____. "Roaring Ahead," *Sports Illustrated*, September 2, 1996

Pierce, Charles P. "The Man. Amen," *Gentleman's Quarterly*, March 1997

Rosaforte, Tim. "Tiger Woods: The Comeback Kid," *Sports Illustrated*, September 5, 1997

Smits, Gary. "Fist Pumping Success," *The Florida Times-Union*, March 23, 1997

Index

Photography Credits

Principal Photography by Allsport USA
©Allsport USA: David Cannon: 11, 28, 44, 45, 74–75, 76, 77, 78, 79, 89, 90, 92–93, 95, 97 both; J.D. Cuban: 12, 13, 30–31, 32, 36, 42–43, 46, 48, 49, 52, 53, 55, 56–57, 57 right, 58, 59, 60, 61, 62, 63, 66, 67, 91; Stephen Dunn: 72, 109; Harry How: 112; Rusty Jarrett: 41; Craig Jones: 6–7, 8–9, 50–51, 64–65, 71, 104–105, 116–117; Alan D. Levenson: 16, 27; Ken Levine: 19; Andy Lyons: 115; Clive Mason: 33; Stephen Munday: 2, 84, 86–87, 99, 102; Gary Newkirk: 18, 20–21, 37, 38; Paul Severn: 73; Jamie Squire: 54, 68; Anton Want: 35

Agence France Presse/Corbis–Bettmann: 80, 82, 83, 88, 96, 100 left, 100–101

©Richard Dole: 14–15, 17, 24 both, 25 both, 26, 29, 34

©Sports Chrome USA: 22; ©David Callow: 108

©Sports Photo Masters: 107, 113; ©Jonathan Eric: 10, 106, 110–111; ©Don Smith: 114

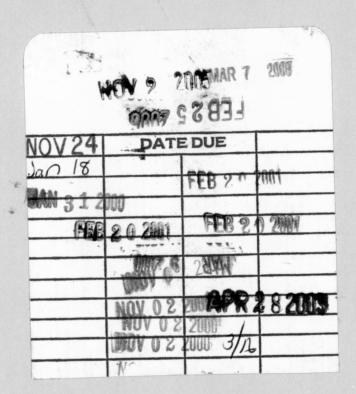